The Brass Ring

How to hire really happy really smart people
(and pay them really well)

Rex W. Castle

Author note: This is a fictional story with predominantly fictional characters, names, places and entities. It is not in any way endorsed by any of the characters or locations mentioned in this work.

The author may be contacted at rcastle263@gmail.com, or through his personal blog at http://hrhiring.wordpress.com/ where a variety of related tools and examples (at no cost) can be found.

The cover art is from a good friend of mine, Dave Conkling. His exceptional work can be seen at www.conklingimages.com. Thanks Dave for the use of you work.

The following is dedicated to my wife, daughter and son-in-law without whom life would not only be far, far different than I ever imagined, but also far less happy—the critical ingredient of all things wonderful.

Contents

Chapter 1
The Chicago Syndrome

"You okay, Mr. Johnson?"

Thomas Johnson, or as most referred to him, 'TJ,' lifted his head from his desk, leaving palm prints on the cherry wood.

Javier Chavez, who, TJ remembered, was somehow or another related to the famous United Farm Worker organizer, stood in the doorway.

"Yep, Javier, just need to head to the house. You have a good night, okay?"

The two ships passing in this night were the recently appointed CEO and the maintenance man who came in after almost everyone was gone and buffed the office back to its morning brilliance. Javier had been around the offices of Trill Industries since the office had opened maybe 20 years before.

"Let me get your jacket, Mr. Johnson."

Before TJ could protest, Javier bounded to the closet, reached in without looking and brought TJ's London Fog overcoat to him.

"There's a bit of a bite in the air, so you'll want this."

TJ shook his head "I sure could use about 250 more just like you, Javier, thanks" he said.

"Ahh, people troubles?"

TJ was a little surprised, a bit taken back, by the immediate acknowledgement and a bit surprised, too, with what came next, "Yep, just challenged at every angle." 'Oh, good,' he thought. 'Now for some wisdom from the maintenance guy.'

"You know Mr. Johnson, you should go visit a friend I met a number of years ago. His name is George..." and he attempted the Greek last name, but fell short. "Well, I still can't pronounce his last name, but he runs a restaurant downtown, Mr. Filet, and besides having the best, and cheapest, lunch specials around, he's surrounded himself with the best people you could possibly imagine. He's got some kind of system."

"Sure thing, Javier," TJ replied. 'Just what I need is cheap E. coli,' he thought. "I'll look at my calendar," TJ said as he finished slipping his tablet into his leather satchel, slung it over his shoulder, unconsciously picked up his Mont Blanc holstering it in his pocket, and headed for the door.

"Have a good night, Mr. Johnson," Javier called after him. "Go see George. I bet he'll have good advice."

TJ waved over his shoulder and hoped Javier wasn't following him to the elevator. The heavy glass door closed behind him and Javier disappeared behind the frosted pane. The clock opposite the wall to the elevator read a little past 8:30. 'Getting out of here early, are you TJ' a little voice in his head said. 'Well, if you were still really married, or had a life, Joyce would be happy to see you before your kids were asleep.'

Really married struck him as unusually cruel even for the little voice that plagued his every move. He and Joyce had separated, or not really separated, but she and the kids were in Chicago and he was in Des Moines and so they weren't here and he wasn't there and separated seemed like the right term. Nothing was official, and they still talked on the phone, and the few weekends he could he was in Chicago. He quieted the little voice in his head by searching his brain for kinder words than *Not Really Married* to describe the story of him and Joyce: separated, but together; married, but separated; geographically apart, but trying to hold it together.

And the little sarcastic voice in his head followed the preceding with 'Sure, right. They're in Chicago. You're in Des Moines. You'll be back together in no time.' The thought made his eyes well with tears.

'Darn it.' he thought.

Even in Des Moines' relatively light traffic the quick trip to his apartment, just off of downtown, was made quicker due to the time. He felt like he could probably easily walk it, but, except for one day, he never had. TJ went out of his way to pull into his favorite, well really only, Chinese joint. "TJ, usual?" Gus, who wasn't really named Gus, but was called that by everyone as his Chinese name was pretty much a string of consonants no westerner could pronounce.

"Extra of that hot sauce, okay?" TJ called back.

"Of course."

The drive from the Chinese place was quick and if TJ hit green lights he could be upstairs at his kitchen table, watching CNN over beef broccoli, sticky and starchy white rice, and deliciously greasy pork wontons in less than 10 minutes.

He had chosen the apartment originally because he was thinking Joyce and Amanda and Lee would be following even though their conversation said different; Joyce didn't want to pull them out of school, then Joyce didn't want to be so far from "home" and then Joyce didn't want to be sitting in some place in Iowa where she knew no one and her husband was more married to his career than to her and their kids. The apartment made sense and the company agreed to pay for it for 6 months and it was nice. He didn't understand either why Joyce was sometimes down on his career.

His career to date had been phenomenal. He hit six figures at 28. He was the youngest EVP ever for Trill Industries. Dr. Anthony "Tony" Trill had pioneered a new learning management social networking site, changing the way people interact with knowledge and sharing collaboratively their thinking on everything from books to videos, and although they weren't Facebook, Google+ or even LinkedIn they had a very nice niche with virtually no competitors in their space and they were growing. Most, importantly, too, they were almost immediately profitable and for an internet concept that was something. The valuation of their business hovered in the upper hundreds of millions and for all intents and purposes TJ was one of the premier future leaders in a company of future leaders. That was until Chicago, but the windy city stumble hadn't exactly killed him either.

He was anxious when Dr. Trill called him personally and asked him to move from their Dallas office to take over their Chicago operation. Chicago was home for Joyce and her parents were ecstatic to hear that the couple and their 'grandbabies' were moving back home.

The Chicago office was smaller than Dallas and it was TJ's first opportunity to lead a diverse group of programmers, web developers salespeople, and marketers. When he arrived, however, he was initially overwhelmed by what had been termed in the company, 'The Chicago Syndrome.'

He had scoffed when his good friend Paul Hines had first mentioned the black hole that was the Chicago operation. An acquisition from a few years back, Chicago had never embraced the rest of the company. They seemed to sit perpetually on the sidelines, never really participating as part of what TJ thought of as a fun and dynamic company.

Even when Dr. Trill held his weekly webinar/teleconference the senior management team in Chicago was noticeably absent—almost always emotionally and more rarely physically.

When Dr. Trill, or Tony as the circle TJ ran in referred to him, called TJ and asked him to assume the helm of Chicago, TJ knew the history, believed maybe half of it and accepted the challenge knowing that Dr. Trill was essentially moving him in and eliminating two of the other top three executives. The original senior management team, however, was far from decimated by this move. In addition to Scott Walker, the CFO, who seemed like a good guy, but a little brusque, there would be holdovers from the past many years. But 'okay,' TJ thought, 'I can deal with them.'

TJ landed in Chicago and his family followed him shortly thereafter. They purchased a house about a block from Joyce's parents and she began unpacking and he began working.

And working.

And working.

The Chicago Syndrome consumed him. The hours required were unrelenting. He felt like he was playing "Whack-A-Mole," but the moles were humans and his aim was off more than it was on...a lot more off than it was on. There simply weren't enough hours in the day. In 18 months TJ could count on one hand the days where he had seen his kids before bedtime. He couldn't remember when Joyce and he had a significant, elongated one-on-one, face-to-face conversation.

TJ took great solace in knowing Joyce had her parents and the kids their grandparents. Then, he was asked to fly to San Francisco to meet with Dr. Trill "about Chicago." 'Rather ominous, don't you think there buddy?' his little voice intoned as he hung up the phone.

'The Chicago Syndrome' spoke to the sense of what was described as 'despair' whenever someone had to have a conversation, a relationship, an interaction with Chicago. TJ had seen it and felt it, but he didn't really understand it until he was there. When he thought about it he thought of darkness. People moped in and at the end of the day they moped out. There was no one in the office much after hours or on weekends; TJ felt he was in a perpetual funeral (and the person in the coffin hadn't even been loved or liked much, and no one was celebrating their life).

Results for Chicago were unremarkably and reasonably fair, but there wasn't a person, it seemed, with his or her heart in the game.

Like drones, they were doing their job.

They were working the required hours.

But they were also brooding and sulking.

Sometimes in the software industry there's a bit of this tendency. Someone has a great idea and someone else gets there first. Many times, too, someone builds the proverbial mousetrap and someone else comes along and builds a much better mousetrap. That's what happened in Dr. Trill's case. He split with some animosity with Corbin Lewis who had started Dynamic Interlude, a company that's basic concept and much of its coding was undeniably, uncomfortably close to Dr. Trill's.

Unfortunately Dr. Trill got the connectivity right and within a few short years Trill swooped back around to Chicago and consumed his old partner's business. The decision Lewis made was simple economics. He could sell to Trill and walk away without a financial worry, or he could fight Trill tooth and nail and watch his company slowly fade away into internet oblivion. He made the right economic decision, but for Chicago they would always be Dynamic Interlude. Thus was born "The Chicago Syndrome."

Lewis left behind people in shock and people in mourning, but people who also held him in highest esteem and what strangely happens in so many acquisition situations the people acquired are upset with the purchasers while the former ownership walk away in great financial shape. Lewis deposited over $72 million and also had a small stake in Trill's ongoing adventure with a respectable 1% of stock and options to purchase a bit more. The entire package obviously set him up for life.

The group he left behind didn't fare as well. Although a "great guy" and "outstanding leader" with a ton of charisma, Lewis was Dynamic Interlude. Unlike Dr. Trill who had a number of people in his inner-circle who he shared the wealth with, Lewis had employees. Friends and close associates for sure, but still employees. When he sold most his friends and associates kept, or chose to keep, their positions, but they had no investment in his company in terms of stock. The customary "thank you" checks many companies hand out to executives following a sale ran in the tens of thousands of dollars with the top being given to Michael Graham, Lewis' closest friend, who Lewis gave a $63,000 bonus "thank you" check to.

None of the preceding numbers, TJ realized, was chump change. His own annual bonus hovered in the $100K range. Adding that to his $172K salary and other perks and Thomas Johnson was doing very, very well. He knew, too, that all the executive management team in Chicago was doing fine financially, but he also knew $72 million was a lot better than $63,000.

And he knew that most the people at the low end of that distribution received checks in the neighborhood of $3,000. One person even received a check for $125 (before taxes) and to TJ that amount was an embarrassment. Mr. Lewis simply didn't share the wealth and apparently saw no need at the point of sale to ask Dr. Trill to take care of Lewis' people. But the curious side of all these numbers and all this financial gobbledygook was that Dr. Trill's company was still there, the Chicago people weren't satisfied and they were very good at demonstrating their extreme dissatisfaction, however misplaced and juvenile that dissatisfaction and animus were.

That's the caustic environment TJ walked into, and like everyone else who had ever been associated with "The Chicago Syndrome," TJ was consumed by it.

Almost immediately he spoke with Marsha Hood, the local HR Manager and asked Marsha to come up with a team building plan. They instigated a revamped bonus plan, scheduled a company picnic and end-of-year party, and Marsha began implementing team building exercises across the various departments. They spent thousands upon tens of thousands of dollars.

The company picnic was attended by maybe 25% of the staff and most the attendees were new since the acquisition. The bonus plan TJ thought was pretty rich, but the extra efforts seemed to be exerted more in the direction of trying to game the system than in trying to hit numbers, cold call goals and developer targets. The team building exercises were of course attended by everyone, many who walked out grumbling things like "what dumb ____ thing would numb nuts come up with next?"

Virtually every initiative he attempted went down in flames and what was burning was cash.

The first 18 months turned into 24 and then turned into 36. And now Dr. Trill wanted to see him in San Francisco... 'face-to-face.'

TJ felt his meteoric career was about to take a markedly different turn, especially when he arrived to see the corporate general counsel in Dr. Trill's office. 'This can't be good,' he thought. However, he arrived to an apology from Dr. Trill.

"TJ, I wanted to start our meeting with an apology." There were a number of people in the meeting in addition to Adrianne Moburg, Corporate Legal Counsel, which TJ, even with the apology, still didn't see as a particularly good sign. "I sort of tossed you in not with the wolves, but with a pack of hungry lions and they pretty much ate you alive. So please accept my apologies."

"No apologies necessary, Tony. I think we're making some inroads in Chicago. I think perhaps we're on the right path."

"TJ, I don't."

Dr. Trill was a lot of things. Blunt and to-the-point were probably most apt descriptors. Honest and forthright were also words TJ had heard in reference to Dr. Trill. He was also decidedly respectful, but many confused his respectfulness as a weakness, which it was anything but.

TJ shifted uncomfortably in his chair.

"You're undoubtedly wondering what that means for you." And after a brief moment, Dr. Trill continued. "TJ, you know John Seymor, in Des Moines, right?"

TJ nodded, vaguely recalling a firm handshake and a gruff voice at a holiday party a few years ago.

"He's retiring at the end-of-the-year. I want to move you over to Des Moines to take John's position leading Des Moines. It's a bit smaller than Chicago. It's also one of our foundation sites, where I started this deal. It's not without its personnel problems, but it's not the inferno that Chicago is."

TJ sort of remembered saying "okay," but he may have said "oh yeah." The wave of relief he felt sort of obliterated the rest of the conversation.

He remember Dr. Trill saying "he'd let Chicago limp along" and he remembered something about "no compensation or bonus structure changes," but he knew because Des Moines was smaller his bonus would take a hit. 'Well my salary even without bonus is way better than zero,' he thought.

He was employed and he really couldn't believe it. He was also more impressed with Dr. Trill's bluntness and honesty than he'd ever been. He was also impressed by Dr. Trill's ability to take ownership of a decision. He had owned the decision to send TJ to Chicago and owned the fact that the decision wasn't probably a good one. Dr. Trill also recognized TJ still had value to add.

TJ knew, too, however, that Des Moines was probably his last chance. Chicago was on Dr. Trill. Des Moines was on TJ.

Dr. Trill had promised an email with a 'Des Moines plan' before TJ left San Francisco, but it didn't arrive until he was about to board his plane very early the following morning. TJ had time to drop the contents into Evernote and quickly save it before being told, again, "sir, please turn that off."

As soon as he could, once the plane reached 10,000 feet, he opened his tablet and accessed 'the plan' Dr. Trill had forwarded to him.

His heart sank as he thumbed immediately to "Financial Projections."

Chapter 2
The Fire

To say the financial projections were aggressive would be a gross understatement. Whereas Chicago was something of a programmer's haven, Des Moines at one time had been the sales flagship. Over the years the sales flagship had become the Dallas office, but, according to the plan, in 36 months, after assuming its head, TJ was looking at double-digit sales goals in a negative growth economy. The plan was for Des Moines to overtake Dallas.

Luckily, he thought, as he closed his eyes he had a few months to work with John Seymor and get his take on what was up with his group, his strengths and weaknesses, maybe even be able to perform a rather involved SWOT (Strengths, Weaknesses, Opportunities and Threats) analysis. 'He could do this,' TJ thought as he drifted off to sleep. 'What's Joyce going to think' was his final thought.

The plane touched down in Chicago jostling TJ awake. He had slept the entire trip and was surprised because although he had been up and down at the hotel the night before he thought he had slept. His tablet had long since gone sound asleep and at some point he'd apparently powered it down, closed its cover and stored it. He hadn't even plugged in his music, so sleeping in the relative turbulence of an airplane was a bit of a new experience. But he recognized the buildings of Chicago's airport zipping by as the plane gradually slowed.

He fumbled in his pocket for his phone and activated it. And unconsciously slid another stack of papers into his briefcase.

He unlocked his phone and the first thing he saw was "Missed Call" and Dr. Trill's office number.

'Rats,' he thought and dialed the call. Dr. Trill's receptionist, Candace, picked up.

"Candace, this is TJ, Tony was trying to get in touch with me, but I was on the..."

"Hold on, TJ." Candace was usually very friendly. TJ hadn't had a lot of conversations with her, but he had talked with her enough to know she wasn't known for her abruptness.

"TJ, Tony," Dr. Trill said. "Listen, I'm on my way to Des Moines. John had a massive heart attack last night and he passed away. I'm going to be there through the funeral. I need you to wrap things up in Chicago in the next 24 hours and then I need you on the ground in Des Moines. Sorry for the push."

TJ remembered saying "okay," or at least he thought he said okay, but Dr. Trill was gone as fast as he was on the phone. Before going to the office and announcing his departure, however, which he thought might actually get his people excited, TJ had one critical conversation he had to have.

He pulled into the driveway. The house he and Joyce, but mostly Joyce, had decided on wasn't all that spectacular. Like most in the neighborhood it was two story and brick. The driveway ran up the side of the house to the side door which opened into the kitchen. He pulled up to the side door and walked in.

"Wow, your home" Joyce said. "Is that a good thing?" The next hour TJ spent filling in Joyce on his last couple of days, his conversation with Dr. Trill, and the phone call from Dr. Trill telling him "the plan" had changed and he was to be in Des Moines essentially tomorrow.

Then Joyce said the word that reverberated in his head virtually every waking moment.

"No."

"I will love you forever, TJ. You've provided for us magnificently over the years, but I need you, not Trill Industries. The kids and I are staying here."

TJ tried to argue, but Joyce said she didn't want to take them out school, then said...the bottom line was that she wanted her kids to be near her parents and she wanted something more than financial support.

Eventually he left for the office confused and dumbfounded and not exactly knowing what his future with his family looked like, but he had to get to the office and close his Chicago operation.

The aura of the funeral TJ felt every time he walked in the door did not improve on his announcement. It was met with a few less than enthusiastic "good lucks," some semi-unimpressive handshakes, but mostly the vacant stares that generally come from the dead. 'Good riddance, then,' TJ thought.

TJ shook his head and then went to his office to get some open items in order. Packing was the quick part of the job. A CFO he had sort of befriended in his career taught him to pack light. "Be ready at a moment's notice for the next thing, son," he had told TJ. "It's the guy who can move the fastest who often gets the promotion." TJ traveled lightly, but that was as much taking the CFO's advice as it was the fact he hadn't been in any one city for more than 3 years.

Plus, his work was coming and going, flying off for a week here and a week there, meeting with customers in one city and meeting with customers later that day in another. He really didn't have a lot of time to accumulate junk in an office. Even in a society and company of hyper-connected people, TJ was hyper-connected.

He was done in an hour and on his way back to the house. Chicago isn't thousands of miles from Des Moines. Unfortunately, he lived near the office and more importantly near Joyce's parents on the east side, so driving through the heart of the city heading west would add at least an hour to a 5 or 6 hour trip.

He packed in relative silence, loaded his car, made one last survey of the upstairs for anything he was missing, grabbing his bedside phone charger and made one last trek downstairs.

"Joyce, I'm outta here, I guess."

"You going to wait for the kids to get home from school?"

"What time do they get home?"

"Amanda's bus is at 3:30 and then we go and pick up Lee and usually get home around 4:45 depending on traffic."

"I better go ahead. I have to be in..."

Joyce stood and held his face in her hands "Tony you're missing a great life to make a good living."

He had to go, though. Des Moines was waiting, Trill was there through the funeral. He had no choice.

She watched him as he tossed the charger onto the passenger seat.

"Tell the kids I love them," he said. He was a bit surprised to be choking back tears.

"I'll try to make it home this weekend."

Joyce looked worn out. She waved plaintively and backed across the threshold and into the house.

Across Chicago was a nightmare. 'I should have just stayed home and waited for this traffic to thin,' he thought. Still he knew he was making some time. The clock in the car showed 9:03 PM by the time he finally cleared most the traffic and was in a wave heading west on I-88 toward Davenport. He was tired, even though he'd slept for much of the day. Perhaps he'd stop in the Quad Cities, Iowa City or even sooner. He had cleared Chicago and so felt he could stop just about anywhere and be a lot closer than where he started.

The next couple of hours he spent thinking about The Chicago Syndrome office, but also formulating a cogent argument for Dr. Trill regarding his possible need for more time to turn Des Moines around. He had just lost the one person who he felt like could help him the most in understanding their issues. He ended up driving straight through, finding a Holiday Inn close to the office and crashing for a couple of hours.

When he arrived, Dr. Trill motioned him into John's old office.

"Listen, services are this afternoon, and then I have to get to New York to meet with some investment guys. Critically important TJ is turning this deal around and doing it at least twice as fast as John's plan I sent you. Too much slippage for too much opportunity, so hit the ground running and don't wait for me. You put in a Chicago-type effort and this deal is going to fly. Great bones."

'So much for asking for time,' TJ thought. "So, 18 months or so," TJ said.

"At the most," Tony responded.

TJ wouldn't know until later in subsequent conversations, but the company was consolidating. Des Moines was home to Dr. Trill and he was rooting for Des Moines to regain its position as the epicenter of Trill Industries, but Dallas was in the "new silicon valley" in the golden triangle of Texas (The Metroplex, San Antonio and Austin) and even Dr. Trill was having trouble seeing how Des Moines could compete for talent, for climate and, most importantly, for cost of wages.

The four major locations Des Moines, Dallas, San Francisco and San Diego would be consolidated to two. Chicago, too, was a major center, but Chicago's acquisition contract forbid relocation or "significant downsizing without a unanimous Board approved argument" for a period of 20 years. Part of the reason Dr. Trill was able to make the deal was that he gave up trying to remove this caveat from a rather unique contract.

TJ missed the services. He didn't know John that well anyway and every minute of every day counted. He had a quick phone call with a real estate person and selected a furnished apartment close to the office, but sight unseen.

Later that afternoon the real estate person dropped off a key and directions to Beth, the receptionist, and TJ had a "home."

TJ worked late that night. He didn't make it home that weekend, or the weekend following that. The effort to turn Des Moines around would take all the energy Dr. Trill had suggested and then some.

Several weeks into the deal, TJ was feeling a level of frustration he hadn't felt since Chicago, but for different reasons. Everyone in Des Moines seemed to be engaged and energetic, hopeful and happy, but they also seemed rudderless, adrift and without direction. TJ was going through his bag of tricks he'd opened in Chicago, but achieving more or less the same results. His time was consumed with the sales group and then he had to turn his attention to operations and then something would come up in accounting. At least the frustration was with happy people.

He was debating whether he needed to make wholesale changes and felt he probably did, but then remembered a conversation he had with Javier a number of weeks before. A conversation about a Greek guy and his restaurant. What was its name? What was his name? TJ wracked his brain. 'George,' he screamed in his head as he came up with the name. 'Mr. Filet,' came another answer shortly after.

'Might as well go see George,' TJ's perpetual little voice intoned. "Might as well," he said out loud and then looked around to ensure no one was within earshot.

Chapter 3
Mr. Filet

TJ had no senior leadership. "Seymor," as the team called TJ's predecessor, managed, or failed to manage, every aspect of the business and didn't let his more tenured people have access to information which was basically required to do their jobs. TJ was disappointed that a man of Seymor's stature in the company wasn't a more progressive thinker, but in TJ's world he always believed reality is sort of what it is. This "foundation in realism" was one of TJ's "rules of success."

TJ had been working on a number of reorganization plans, shuffling people around. He'd spoken with Javier on a number of occasions about strengths and weaknesses of individuals. TJ looked up from his desk. He realized he had just been thinking about 'his advisor,' the 'custodian' and wanted to be sure he hadn't said anything out loud that anyone would have heard. Apparently he hadn't, or at least no one seemed to have been close enough to hear if he had.

But Javier wasn't what TJ thought of as a maintenance man, although truth be known he really hadn't ever thought twice about maintenance people. They were always sort of the invisible people who came into a shadowy building after hours and emptied the trash, vacuumed the hallways, buffed the entryway and cleaned the restrooms. He didn't think he even knew any of their names. He thought about it for a moment and thought one of them in Chicago might have been named Sally or maybe Susan, but he wasn't sure.

He saw her face in his mind's eye, but no name attached itself to her face. He felt a moment's pause. 'I wonder if they could have provided all the insight Javier has been able to provide?' he thought. 'I wonder if I should have known their names?'

A few weeks before Javier had told TJ about Mr. Filet and George. TJ hadn't been to visit George and didn't know what some Greek guy who ran a restaurant would be able to tell him about selling software and services for a collaborative learning community, but lunch was approaching, his calendar was remarkably clear, and so TJ thought he'd head downtown and see if he could find the place.

Finding the place wasn't hard. It sits under the parking garage on 7th Street. The line stretched out the door, but the day was nice, if a bit breezy and he took his place at the end of the queue, which rather quickly became the middle of the line. He could hear George and knew it was him because some of his customers called him by name. His accent wasn't heavy, but it was pronounced and as he received an order he'd repeat the order back.

"Special, medium rare, got it. Thanks."

"Shrimp, steak burger, got it. Thanks."

"No, he'll get your potato."

"Pay at the end."

"Here, take tray. Silverware here, salad in there."

"Yes, chicken gets salad, it in there. Salad extra with sandwich."

TJ smiled. He liked Javier, but he was out of his mind if he thought George could help him with his personnel issues.

It was his turn. He hadn't looked at the menu board, as he'd been consumed by the assembly line in front of him.

"Tuesday, Special, rib-eye, $6.50."

"Sounds good," TJ said.

"How do you want it cooked?" George asked.

"Hmm..."

"Medium rare is best."

"Okay."

"Take tray, silverware, salad in there."

Before TJ knew it the queue moved him to in front of the salad dressing, which you ladled out on your own salad, and another, Greek, a younger man than George asked him "baked or fries?"

"What," TJ asked.

"Baked potato or French fries?"

The younger man had no accent, but his dark hair and eyes said to TJ "Greek."

"Fries," TJ wondered why he ordered fries when he almost always ate a baked potato.

"Anything to drink?" a tall, slender man asked, punching TJ's order into the register's keypad without even looking down at the buttons.

"Can I get a coke?" TJ asked.

"You can get anything you pay for," the man smiled. His accent was more pronounced than George's, and he, too, was obviously Greek.

By the time TJ had paid, another minute or so, the kid who had talked to him about his potato choice deftly put his meal in front of him. 'Wow, that was quick,' TJ thought.

"Thank you," the kid said as he drew back his arm and TJ noticed a broad smile on his face. TJ, who generally wasn't all that observant had watched the staff, after all he was here to talk with George about his own staff, and from

George to the busboys everyone seemed to be smiling, or, if they weren't smiling, they all appeared to be 'happy.'

'Well, if they were in the Chicago office, that wouldn't last,' TJ thought and made his way to a small table toward the back of the restaurant.

TJ sat and ate and watched for a little bit. The line out the door dwindled momentarily and he took that opportunity to go back up to the register.

"Can I help you?" the tall slender guy who had taken his money asked.

"Could I steal a minute from George?" TJ asked.

The tall slender guy, who TJ would find out was named Simeon (se moan), yelled from the register something that sounded like "Yor-gi, coon-a-stone-go-lo-sue. Ma-lock-a."

In Greek, the yell sounded less like a shout and more like music. But either way George was beside the register in short order.

"George, I'm TJ, Jav…"

George interrupted "Yes, yes, Javier told me about you. Come back at 2:30 today. I can't talk now" and he turned with his perpetual smile and went back to work.

TJ counted them as he walked out of the place. There were two busboys, Simeon, the baked or fries kid and George and he received six "thank yous" before he left the restaurant. He figured he must have gotten a thank you from a customer. He peered in through the front window of the restaurant as he walked past. George waved from the grill at the start of the speed line and again TJ noticed the smiles.

He knew he had a meeting at 2:00 that would last most the afternoon, so he also knew that George's desire to have him come back at 2:30 wasn't a real possibility. 'Oh, well,' he thought 'great lunch anyway.'

The meeting that afternoon was more of the bloodbath he'd sort of become accustomed to. Des Moines' numbers placed them squarely on the bottom in terms not just of their rival Dallas, but of every other location, even some half their size. TJ was embarrassed by their performance and vowed again to do something about it.

"Hey, Javier, how's your evening?" he asked seeing Javier outside his door.

"Obviously better than yours appears to be, Mr. Johnson," Javier responded.

"Yep, another day in paradise."

"Whassup?" Javier asked plopping himself in one of the comfortable chairs at TJ's conference table.

TJ smiled at how easy their relationship had become and smiled again when he realized he was about to once again share with the maintenance man his concerns about this division.

"Oh, Javier, I don't know. My team hasn't any energy in the right direction. I don't know if they don't care or they've decided they can't be successful. I've tried incentives, threats, begging..." TJ went on sharing with Javier his ideas for reorganization and his thoughts on the personalities he was working with and his thoughts and concerns about all the various obstacles in his way.

Javier listened intently, sometimes nodding his head and sometimes confirming TJ's perception of his team and occasionally disagreeing with him. They talked late into the evening.

"Oh, my gosh," TJ finally said, "I am so sorry. I've taken up your whole evening and put you behind."

"No worries, Mr. Johnson," Javier said, "I was in early today and got most everything except your office done."

"Leave mine, Javier."

"Naw, I'll get it."

"Can I ask you one thing?"

"Mr. Johnson, you're the boss, you ask me anything you want."

"What do you think?"

Javier leaned against the doorframe and didn't say anything immediately, letting the question wash over him. "Well, probably you don't have the right people in the right seats on the bus. I read that in *First Break All the Rules*, I think, by the way. And you may have a few people who don't belong on the bus. And then you need to find some folks who can drive the bus. Did you ever go talk to George?"

"I went down there the other day, but he was too busy and then my afternoon was a mess and I couldn't go back, so we missed one another."

"Go tomorrow. Go at 1 or 1:30. The rush is usually done around then and you can have something to eat and wait for George. He'll clean up a bit and then come and talk with you. Tell him just what you told me tonight and see what he says. Mr. Johnson, that's the best advice I can give you. Oh, and call your wife. You need to talk with her about this stuff too and find out how her world is."

With that Javier was out the door.

'Talk to George. That was it,' TJ thought. This George guy must be something. But what was 'call your wife' all about? He'd probably tell Javier that was a little over the line. They had a different sort of relationship, but TJ felt there was still a line. 'Wasn't there?'

He picked up the phone and dialed home.

Chapter 4
Different View

TJ left the office early for lunch the next day. He knew George would be too busy to talk, but he had his tablet and he would wait. His conversation with Joyce the night before spurred him, not by anything she said, but by something she didn't: "I'm coming with the kids to Des Moines." He realized in talking with her and saying a brief "hell-o" to Amanda and Lee how badly he missed his family.

'Perhaps absence does make the heart grow fonder,' he thought. He knew the only way to get her to consider Des Moines was for him to demonstrate success and the ability to stay in one place for more than a couple of years. She'd been the rock to his children and to him and he could understand her not wanting to move again, but if he could show the move was something a bit more permanent than a few years, who knew?

The line was shorter today. George was taking orders.

"Good morning, TJ," George said as he approached. "Rib-eye, medium rare?" George asked.

"Sure," TJ eventually answered, a little surprised George remembered him, but George seemed to remember everyone.

"Missed you the other day," George said over the sizzling grill.

"Yeah, uh, sorry," TJ mumbled. "Had a meeting I couldn't get out of."

"Well, you're here now, but I'm about to get busy. Can you come back later today?"

"No, but I'm just going to wait for you."

"May be a bit."

TJ waved George off. "I'll be here."

TJ really didn't know what else to do. He didn't like the multiple plans he'd tried and the multiple plans he'd put in place, or the multiple plans he was still messing with. He didn't like the thought of a massive reorganization and displacing some long-term workers and hiring new ones who probably wouldn't know the business before his dwindling timeframe was up. So TJ guessed he was really here in a speed line, in a small Greek steakhouse, under a parking garage, in Des Moines, Iowa because he was that desperate.

'That's pretty desperate,' he thought as he made his way through mostly empty tables.

The lunch rush didn't seem to want to end and so the time was approaching three in the afternoon before George finally came over, shook TJ's hand and sat down.

"Oh, wait, let me get you another coke," George said and before TJ could say he'd had enough George was off.

TJ laid out what he had done. He told George about the multiple plans he'd tried. He got a little frustrated as every now and then George would have to get up to order the potatoes for tomorrow, or inventory something being delivered to the restaurant, and there was a steady stream of customers that stopped by "to chat."

And then TJ would have to endure their history.

But George accommodated all of it seemingly effortlessly and always seemed completely focused on the moment in front of him. 'Amazing,' TJ thought and through it all TJ walked George through Trill Industries' story and TJ's successes and failures, triumphs and frustrations.

George sat silently across from him with that perpetual smile on his face.

After TJ finished and after what seemed to be a few minutes of silence TJ asked "So what do you think?"

George smiled and began. "You need to hire a sales manager, a VP of Sales, someone to lead that team."

"But I lead that team," TJ protested.

"Yes, that's wrong," George said. "You can't lead that team and manage the organization. They both need someone full-time, so you need a senior guy reporting to you and you need to get out of that day-to-day."

"Ok, so I post the position and hire someone," TJ said frustration in his voice.

"Who are you going to hire?" George asked.

"What?"

"Who are you going to hire?"

"I don't know. I'll get HR to post something and I'll hire somebody to take over the sales function."

"If you always do what you always done, you'll always get what you always got," George said and smiled "there's a customer from the *Register* that taught me that."

"Yeah, I've heard it," TJ said gathering his things.

"What are you going to hire?" George asked.

"What?"

"What are you going to hire?"

"A VP of Sales, I guess. Maybe a Director. I'll see what resumes I get."

"Sit," George said. It wasn't a command, but it wasn't a question either. TJ sat back down.

"You cannot hire based off what some job description says and what HR gives you. If you do you maybe will have a 50% or 60% chance of hiring what you need. Is that good enough for you?"

"Absolutely not. But what are you talking about?"

"Who are the best sales managers you know at Trill or otherwise?"

"Good question," TJ responded. "I guess I'd start with Craig Peraccilli and Don Nixon. And there's hmmm…Lori Lennon overseeing our southeast region, Michael Bangs at Microsoft, Doug…"

By the time George and TJ had finished with the question TJ had a list of eleven names.

"Now," George said, "you want to know what makes each successful."

TJ began "Craig has this team under him that just blows everyone away, so he's a great team builder. Don's a hoot, so I'd say having a sense of humor would be important and Lori is way organized…"

George laughed. "Wait, TJ. Your success is an impediment. You have the 'Curse of Knowledge,'" George finished.

'Wow,' TJ thought. 'Curse of Knowledge from the Heaths' *Made to Stick*; this is no normal restaurant owner.'

"I'm confused," TJ said.

"Okay," George began, "you are successful, you've been in this industry for a few years, you know all the acronyms and the jargon, but you're viewpoint is constrained by where you sit. What you can see is blocked by the view you know is there. You cannot, therefore, define what you need because you think you know what it is you need. You have to ask."

"Ask what?"

"You have to ask the sales managers, the superstars you list, what it is that makes them so successful."

"All of them?"

George smiled.

"You put them in priority order of who you think is absolutely best and you call the first one and you simply say 'The reason I am calling to talk with you is I believe you to be an exceptional sales manager and I want to get a better idea as to why. So, I'm here to try to define what it is you do differently than even perhaps your peers that makes you so successful. In that vein please describe for me your day and your interactions with your clients and anything you might see, or think, you do differently.' And, then, TJ your job is to listen and take notes."

TJ was typing furiously into Evernote.

"What comes after 'So, I'm here to try to define what,' George. I couldn't keep up."

George repeated himself and TJ, typing furiously again, finally captured the essence of George's question.

"Okay, I got it."

"TJ," George said and waited for TJ to look at him, "you have to listen and take notes after that. Really, really copious notes. What you will find probably by the time you get to your second interview is that some of the things the first person you talk with will be repeated in some form or fashion by your second interview and then by your third."

"Okay, George, no problem."

"When you get to your fourth or fifth interview, you'll find you're writing less and less because they're simply confirming the preceding interviews. And, then, too, you can stop. You have what you need."

TJ nodded his head. "Okay, George...What will I have?"

George chuckled. "You'll see, TJ. There'll be four or five primary attributes that all your superstars use when they're being successful. Those attributes, then are what you'll build your questions around and ask the people you interview to determine if they have what is required to do the job. You are building a composite model of the most successful superstars performing in a position. To do this successfully, though, TJ, will require you to control your preconceived notions of what you think this composite looks like."

"Can you help me with the questions?"

"I'd be happy to, but you can't write the questions until you know what you're looking for."

"I'm on it," TJ responded, gathered his things and exited the restaurant.

'Wow, wow, wow,' TJ thought. 'How cool is this?' And then he caught himself smiling and looked around to ensure no passersby thought he had lost his mind.

'Wait a minute,' TJ thought to himself, 'I'm excited about hiring? Is that even possible?' and he smiled again. 'How cool.'

The next couple of days TJ had his head down. He cancelled most his meetings and didn't return most phone calls. His email box filled to some degree. He interviewed Craig, then Lori, and then Michael and as George had suggested by the time he got to Michael TJ had mostly quit taking notes.

TJ had more than four or five attributes, but he wasn't overly concerned. In no particular order TJ wrote down his list incorporating some of his thoughts:

Great sales managers—

>...see themselves in the future, their company position, market share, etc...

>...listen actively and are intellectually curious, read all the time and hire similar...

>...are action oriented, quickly attacking problems and just as quickly making decisions, realizing results count and intentions and excuses do not...

>...have a strong commitment to building a team of confident, competent, happy people who will tell the great sales manager the truth...

>...walk the walk, commanding respect by their example and living what they teach...

Those TJ decided were his top five. He was leaning toward making "have a strong commitment to building a team" his number one, but he wanted George's input before ordering his list. Then he decided to write down his next group, which he envisioned were "the separators." What he saw "the separators" doing was moving a candidate up or down his list.

TJ continued his notes, now capitalizing "GREAT:"

And GREAT sales managers—

> ...promote reasonable risk taking, after action reviews (AARs) and bounce back quickly...

> ...embrace change...

> ...are really good at hiring, training, recruiting and retaining great people...

TJ looked at the list and was impressed. The process had worked and he felt very comfortable he now knew what he needed for his role. Funny, too, he felt like he could develop questions pretty easily that would test for many of the attributes he'd discovered.

Javier was in his doorway.

"Hey, Mr. Johnson," Javier said. "When did you go home last?"

"Javier," TJ said "great to see you. How are you doing? Thanks for George. He's a goldmine?"

"When did you last eat?" Javier asked.

"You've got to look at this. Look at what I've come up with. I hate hiring and this process is just way cool."

"Mr. Johnson, you need to get some sleep."

"Not yet, Javier. I've got to get to the restaurant."

"Mr. Johnson, it's closed. It's after 10. You need to go home now."

TJ couldn't sleep. He kept mulling over and over the interviews he'd done, all the great information he'd been given. He called Joyce.

Amanda and Lee were asleep and Joyce had been. TJ apologized to his wife.

"I had to talk with someone," he said and then realized that probably wasn't the best way to start a conversation with someone who wasn't exactly a fan and who you also just woke up.

"Okay, that didn't come out that great, but something incredible is happening here in Iowa. Can you come over here for a few days?"

The phone was quiet.

"You don't have to stay, but I gotta show you some stuff. You need to meet George and Javier, you know there the guys, well, Javier anyway, I've told you about, but George is great too. You know the maintenance guy and the restaurant guy, the Greek guy. And, Joyce, wow, I've learned so much. And I miss you and the kids and I need to fix that I know and I need you and we need to talk stuff out, so maybe your mom and dad could keep the kids for a few days and you could hop a flight over here and...well, okay, all that I just said I'm not sure where all that came from, but can you come over?"

The phone stayed quiet.

"Joyce?" TJ asked into the phone.

"Joyce!" TJ elevated his voice a bit.

"Hell-o," came a sleepy response.

"I love you," TJ said. "I'll call you tomorrow. Sorry for waking you."

"K, love you too."

The phone went silent.

'Love you too' sang in TJ's head.

'This had been a good day,' TJ thought and turned back to his list of attributes. 'This is so cool,' he repeated to himself and remarkably it was late Saturday morning before he had another conscious thought as physically and emotionally exhausted he had closed his eyes for "just a moment" and the moment had turned into a long good night's sleep.

Chapter 5
Detour

Joyce was coming. He'd caught her before she went to pick up Amanda from a friend's house she went to after dance and was able to have a rather disjointed conversation with Lee in the background, but she had somewhat reluctantly agreed to come. Later she would call back with flight information, arriving Monday and leaving Wednesday. Not much time, but TJ knew he could have her meet the two important people in this new world he'd found.

TJ didn't get to the office until mid-afternoon Saturday and then when he got there he wasn't sure why he came in. He tried to catch up on emails, but he kept going back to his analysis of the GREAT sales manager. He couldn't leave it. 'This may not solve anything,' he thought, 'but, wow, what an experience to take to his next job.' He didn't want a next job, but he was now several months into this adventure and he'd made exactly zero progress on achieving any of his goals and had made exactly zero progress on developing a plan to achieve his goals.

Well, none of that was true. He'd actually developed, tried and discarded multiple plans. Similar to, but dissimilar to, Chicago, he had tried and retried a bunch of things. Nothing seemed to budge the numbers. In Chicago he got the distinct sense that no one cared; in Des Moines he felt as though he hadn't hit the right button yet. Maybe this thing he was working on with George. 'Maybe this thing he was working on with George...' he thought. 'Yes, Dr. Trill, Ph.D., the Greek immigrant restaurant owner...'

He sunk in his chair. 'What are you doing TJ?' he thought to himself.

"Mr. Johnson, Mr. Johnson. You're here today. I didn't think you were in. I thought maybe you actually were taking a day off," said Javier pushing his cart into TJ's office.

"Javier," TJ said.

"Sir?"

"Why won't you call me TJ?"

"You're my boss Mr. Johnson. I respect the position you have and I respect you. I like to call you Mr. Johnson."

"What can I do to change that? I appreciate the respect, but I consider us less boss and subordinate and more friends."

"My friends come to my house for dinner."

TJ looked up. "How about Tuesday night?"

Sunday seemed to drag on into perpetuity. TJ tried to answer emails, but the excitement of the preceding week and the fact Joyce was coming was overwhelming. He quickly went down his inbox and simply deleted the majority of things that didn't look to be all that important.

He'd never done anything like that in his career and he felt sort of giddy and kind of 'little kid naughty.' He left the Brownstones on Grand and walked over to the Principal Riverwalk. The Brownstones were great for his needs. They were a bit pricey for his taste, but the company was picking up the tab still, so he wasn't overly concerned. He hadn't told anyone that Joyce had told him she was staying in Chicago. He had told everyone, well Javier on Saturday, she was coming in "next week." He thought about that as he made the turn toward the river.

He hoped maybe this coming week would convince Joyce that she and the kids needed to join him Des Moines. He wasn't real hopeful, but he hoped.

Joyce arrived late Monday afternoon.

He met her as she cleared the restricted area of the airport. They held their hug for a long time and then he grabbed her roller bag and they headed to the car. He had so much he wanted to tell her, but found himself struggling to make much sense of it all. He wanted to tell her how much this adventure had changed him, but didn't know exactly how to say "and now I have a Greek immigrant friend" and "we're eating at the Spanish guy's house tomorrow," so instead their conversation devolved into a discussion of Amanda's dance class and Lee's shenanigans.

He did bring up Javier and the plan to go to his house to meet his family and have dinner tomorrow night. And he talked some about George and Mr. Filet and Joyce was excited to go with TJ to the restaurant, but was a little surprised to hear George wasn't open in the evening. After TJ ran her bag up to the apartment—she wanted to "take in downtown," which TJ thought was a good sign—they spent the early evening wandering around downtown and eventually stopped at Lucca's for some Italian and then headed back to the Brownstones.

"Wow," Joyce said as the door opened.

"You've been sort of living the life of luxury, haven't you?"

TJ smiled. He'd become accustomed to the Brownstones, but they really were quite opulent.

"They are really nice, aren't they?" he said.

"Sort of like a Jaguar is a 'really nice' car," she chided.

He was a little embarrassed. He knew their home in Chicago paled by comparison, even though it didn't have to. TJ had always been frugal, or as Joyce would say "cheap," and so the Brownstones amplified the disparity.

They talked late into the night and after one of his power naps TJ left her asleep as he headed to the office. He wrote out a note, "Joyce, I love you. Thank you for making the trek to Iowa for me. Hopefully you don't mind making the short trip to my office by yourself. There's almost always a cab downstairs, or if you feel like it, the walk is not strenuous," and then he printed out instructions to get to his office "whenever." He knew he needed some time with George to talk about his interviews, but he also knew if he consumed their lunch or their dinner with work he and Joyce were probably done.

Joyce called a little bit before 11 to tell TJ she was heading toward his office. He elected to meet her and then they could walk together over to the restaurant. He still didn't know how he would get some time with George, but maybe if he paid attention to Joyce until George was free that would be enough to sneak in a few minutes.

Joyce arrived at the office before TJ left, so rather than meet her, as had been his plan, she and TJ did the obligatory office tour. He introduced her to as many employees as he knew, but realized he really didn't know very many and opened Evernote on his tablet and typed a note.

"What are you writing?" Joyce asked.

"A note to myself. I'm realizing walking around with you that I don't know a lot of these folks and that's not right. I need to make more of an effort to get to know these people."

"Really?" she said and he looked up to see her staring at him, but with what he perceived to be an approving look.

'Okay, another good moment,' he thought and returned her smile.

They walked over to Mr. Filet. The air had an unseasonable slight nip to it and TJ could see the leaves on the few trees in the downtown area starting to turn.

"Fall's coming," he said to no one in particular.

"Yeah, it's pretty much in full swing at home."

'...at home,' he thought. 'Not a good moment.' He realized, too, that without anyone sitting in his office and pointing it out. Time was passing. When he arrived the weather was moving from cooler to warmer and now the cycle was reversing itself. He erased that pressure as best as he could, but a more pronounced pale now hung over him.

The restaurant was already slammed and the wait was longer than usual.

'...another not good moment,' he thought. 'Three strikes and you're out.'

And then the wind started to pick up and air went from 'a bit of a nip' to 'cold.'

'Third strike?' he thought.

"Just like Chicago," Joyce said.

'...not a good or bad moment, but hurry up, George.'

"Hey, TJ," George called from behind the cooktop. "Whose that you got with you."

TJ hollered back "George, this is Joyce, my..."

"Oh, you're better half. We get to meet the famous Joyce at last. I didn't think you were real he talks about you so much," George hollered.

'Good moment, George, way to go,' TJ thought, but couldn't really remember having ever said much of anything about Joyce or the kids.

"So, you're the one bringing up two wonderful kids for this guy, eh?" George said as he extended his hand and shook hers.

She smiled, "I guess so."

TJ was monumentally confused as he knew he hadn't talked but maybe for a moment about his family with George, but George seemed to know them intimately. 'I'll have to ask George about that. Maybe Javier has talked about them,' TJ thought, but was trying to keep stray thoughts to a minimum and focus on Joyce.

"Ah, Ms. Bridget Bardot," Simeon said from down the speed line. He called every woman he couldn't remember Bridget Bardot and the Bridget came out more Brid-jeet, but his greeting still brought a wide smile to Joyce's face.

"How fun," she whispered to TJ.

'...more good moments.'

"Two specials," George asked and TJ looked at Joyce and she shrugged her shoulders. "Why not?" she asked.

Without realizing, George had changed his Tuesday specials to gyros (pronounced e-rows with light emphasis on the e, almost as though there were a small breathless h in front of the e—most Americans pronounced the dish ji-row, but that pronunciation was way wrong). Traditional gyros are made with thinly shaved lamb, but for Americans most gyros have a majority of beef in them and George's were no different.

"I buy today, Simeon," George yelled.

"Okay, okay. We not make any money though."

"It's okay," George yelled back.

'How incredibly wonderful,' TJ thought. 'What could be better?'

TJ and Joyce sat through the lunch hour and finally George made his way to the table.

"So, how were the gyros?"

"I didn't realize the special changed," TJ said.

"Delightful," Joyce said. "I had never had one."

George then went into an explanation of gyros, their history and consistency.

"Joyce, if you're okay with it, I need to talk to George for a minute about that deal I told you about that he and I are working on."

Joyce looked out the window. "Sure, T. Whatever you need."

"Nah," George said. "I'll come by your office tomorrow after Joyce leaves" (TJ couldn't remember telling George when Joyce would be leaving). "Remember, TJ, we already set that appointment."

TJ pulled out his calendar, clicked it on, but couldn't find the appointment. He looked up at George who was sitting slightly behind Joyce. George was waving his hand back and forth, signaling "no" to TJ. He also wore an expression on his face TJ could best describe as "pained."

TJ got the hint. "Oh...um...I guess I simply forgot to calendar it, George. My bad." He typed "George" on his calendar at no particular time and put his phone back in his pocket.

After some light conversation and bantering with Simeon, George stood, "Ms. Joyce, very nice to meet you. Thank you so much for waiting on me." At that George extended his hand, shook Joyce's and moved back to his work.

As they were exiting the restaurant Simeon shouted "See you Ms. Brid-jeet Bardot" and Joyce smiled and waved back.

"I can see why you like that place. Those guys are a riot," Joyce said.

"Yeah, there a couple of good ones," TJ said and wondered when he'd have a chance to catch up with George as time was most critical. "Really smart too."

Joyce hung around the office for most the afternoon and then headed back to the apartment.

"Things going okay, Mr. Johnson."

"A good day so far, Javier. How about you?"

"Going good. Family is looking forward to meeting you tonight."

TJ realized his visit to Javier's home would be the first time he'd ever stepped out of his executive management circle for an evening out. He wasn't sure this was a good move, a kosher step. The CEO and the maintenance guy hobnobbing around Des Moines might not sit well with Dr. Trill.

'Knock it off TJ,' he thought to himself. 'It's a dinner at Javier's home for crying out loud.'

"We'll see you then." TJ tossed a couple of stacks into his satchel. It was just before 4. He couldn't remember a day when he was leaving the office before dark. He felt oddly guilty. There were a lot of firsts making him feel this way lately.

But he also knew he had to show Joyce he'd made some changes.

As he walked to the elevator he also wondered how Javier always managed to be around the office anytime he needed him. 'Oh, well,' TJ thought. 'His business.'

When TJ opened the door to the apartment he could hear the shower running. 'Hmm,' he thought. 'A good day? Perhaps he shouldn't push his luck.'

Chapter 6
Decision

Javier lived in Urbandale. His home was maybe a 20 to 25 minute drive from the apartment. He had asked TJ and Joyce to "come over" around 7:30. Joyce had stopped on her way back to the apartment and picked up a wine gift basket. TJ thought that a bit over-the-top, but he was walking on eggshells, trying to make this visit perfect, and so embraced the whole idea.

Joyce was still working on her face as the clock ticked to 7:10. TJ paced by the door, sat on the couch and then got up to go into the bathroom and see how things were going.

Before he could make what he was feeling would be a disastrous move, however, Joyce appeared wrapped in a towel. "Where does the time go?" she said and scurried off to the bedroom.

"No problem," and TJ could feel a bit of perspiration forming around his collar and began seeking alternate routes in his mind. 'Okay, if I can get out of the garage, hit all the lights just right and…'

At that moment Joyce whirled around the corner.

"Done," she exclaimed.

Her blue dress flowed effortlessly down to mid-thigh and a single strand of pearls he'd given her for her birthday 3 years before was the perfect accent.

He stood for a moment. "You look amazing," he said.

She smiled, "Thank you. That's always nice to hear." and he found himself running out the door to catch her.

He heard the door lock behind him as he remembered his billfold and keys sitting on the kitchen table.

And he saw himself in his mind's eye turning in slow motion and groaning 'n-o-o-o-o-o,' but it was too late. As he grabbed the door handle it simply went up and down seemingly agreeable to move in this fashion and accomplish nothing for eternity.

He groaned.

"What's wrong?" Joyce asked.

TJ had his forehead resting against the door. "My keys and billfold are on the kitchen table. Door's locked."

"That's not good," Joyce said.

"No, not good," he responded.

"Want to use my key?" Joyce asked after a number of long, quiet seconds.

TJ had forgotten early on he'd sent Joyce a key to the apartment. He hadn't thought when she left him at the office "how did she get in?" There wasn't much reason in his mind that he remembered to think she'd ever need the key, want it, or use it, but at the moment he didn't care to debate his memory.

He turned to see his beautiful wife, smiling and holding out the key.

"All things are good, TJ."

"You know, of course, don't you," TJ said, "that, that wasn't that funny." They both shared the laugh as he entered the apartment, walked to the kitchen, took a deep breath, exhaled, picked up his keys and billfold and also remembered to grab the gift basket as he walked out the door.

"Oh, the wine basket. Good one," Joyce said and they made their way to the elevator.

"We do pretty good together, TJ," she said.

'A good moment,' he thought and some of the pressure he was feeling and his general lack of sleep sort of melted away.

From there being a few minutes late to Javier's didn't seem like a big deal any longer. They hit every green light, so TJ figured they were making up time, and he also quietly acknowledged his life had truly changed as he couldn't remember the last time he'd hit all greens.

Javier's lawn was immaculate. Even in the waning light of the day, that was the first thing TJ noticed. Everything in its place. The home was very much similar in size to their Chicago place. They walked up the ramp to the front door and rang the bell.

"Hi, I'm Crystal," the lady in wheelchair said as she extended her hand. TJ stood looking down at Crystal. Javier had never mentioned his wife being in a wheelchair. Actually, he'd never asked Javier about his wife, his kids, his life. 'What a jerk I am,' TJ thought. Joyce sort of moved him aside and took Crystal's hand.

"I'm Joyce. This is TJ."

"Welcome to our home."

At that moment a boy, maybe 4 years old came racing around the corner and slid across the hardwood floor, crashing into the wall.

He quickly scrambled to his feet, "To eternity!" he shouted.

"Angel," Crystal scolded softly.

"Sorry, mom," the boy shouted, picking up a disheveled Buzz Lightyear. "...and beyond," he yelled and ran off.

"Don't make me come after you," Crystal shouted after him.

"You can't. I'm going to the basement."

"No lift," Crystal looked up at her guests.

"Javier is in the kitchen, so come on in."

Javier came through the entryway to the kitchen. "Hey, TJ, good to see you."

'Hey TJ...' rang in his head and he thought 'TJ! Perfect.'

"You must be Javier," Joyce said and reached for his hand, but Javier gave her a big hug.

"And you must be what keeps Mr. Johnson's blood pumping," Javier said as he embraced Joyce. "TJ talks incessantly about you and Amanda and Lee."

And, like with George, TJ tried to recall the "incessant" conversations Javier was referencing, but none came to mind, and he tried to remember the last time, or if, he'd actually told Javier his kids' names.

There were two other kids in the Chavez house and one at college, four in all. The oddity and discomfort TJ felt seeing Crystal in a wheelchair disappeared in short order. Sort of like his initial discomfort he had felt for his friend, Javier based on the silly factors of Javier's station in life and also, embarrassingly, and to a limited degree, on his race. He felt uncomfortable with Crystal in a wheelchair now with his initial discomfort and 'what a jerk' pounded in his head like a tireless drummer.

'What a jerk, you've been' and then his brain started composing a list of all the people he'd been a jerk toward over the years, and included on that list were Joyce, Amanda and Lee. He was a bit amazed, actually, at how many times Joyce and Amanda and Lee showed up on the list. Dinner and drinks were delightful full of stories and laughter. The kids eventually went off to another part of the house and only occasionally could a "to eternity," or something similar be heard. Eventually, the night wound down.

"TJ, I'm sorry, but I all of a sudden just got a case of the 'I'm overwhelmingly tired,'" Joyce whispered in TJ's ear. TJ, too, was feeling the strain of the last few weeks on him.

"Don't want to overstay our welcome," TJ said to Javier. "Let's do this again sometime."

"Soon, I hope," Crystal said.

There were the obligatory "good-byes" and "nice to meet yous." Joyce instinctively bent down to give Crystal a hug and TJ sort of awkwardly followed her lead. Then, TJ and Joyce were back in his car heading to their apartment.

"Nice couple," he said. "Nice family."

"I'm sorry, TJ. I don't know what came over me."

"No thing."

Joyce was leaving the next day and TJ and her had skirted the proverbial elephant in the room and now she seemed genuinely exhausted and in need of sleep, but TJ had to know.

As Joyce crawled into bed, TJ asked the question.

"So, what do you think?"

"Huh?" was all Joyce said.

"About this? About Des Moines? About us? Maybe you guys considering a move here?"

"I love you," was all TJ received in return and Joyce was out.

'I wonder what that meant?' he thought rolled out of bed, and went to pick up some emails and get some work finished.

'Geez,' he thought as his inbox came up.

He worked late into the night, or early into the morning depending on perspective, but remarkably he couldn't sleep anyway.

Joyce had a plane to catch and was running around most the morning. TJ was tired but he got up anyway and tried to stay out of her way. He was looking for an opening. He tossed her bag in the car and they pulled out of the parking lot. The ride to the airport seemed awkward. He didn't say much and she didn't either.

Finally, at the airport he asked again.

"TJ, I love you. You seem to be making changes and I think Des Moines has been good for you. Gosh, I never would have thought you would have a friend like Javier or one like George, but…"

The 'but' hung there in his mind for a moment under the pile of crushed hope.

"…the kids and I are staying in Chicago. We'll wait for you there."

And then she was gone, and for the first time in his history of flying TSA actually seemed to move quickly and in the briefest of moments she disappeared through security.

He sat down in a monumentally uncomfortable airport chair and watched her plane lumber down the runway, gradually picking up speed and then thunder into the air and disappear off into the clouds above the horizon. He continued to stare at the clouds until the place the plane had disappeared into itself disappeared under a darkening sky. He returned to his car with tears welling in his eyes. He knew he had another decision to make.

Chapter 7
The Final Piece

TJ took everything he felt he might need to the restaurant the following day. Joyce leaving weighed heavily on him, but he had to finish the job he'd started. To do otherwise was career suicide. Lunch was remarkably light and so George joined him earlier than usual.

George asked about dinner at Javier's and TJ once again found himself racking his brain trying to remember when George and he had talked about dinner at Javier's. 'The guy has a memory,' TJ thought.

They exchanged some other pleasantries and then TJ, impatient, walked George through the people he'd talked with and the contacts he'd made.

"Okay, this is good," George said. "Now tell me what you are looking for."

TJ was ready he pulled out his job description and handed it to George. TJ realized he'd pretty much plagiarized from several he found at monster and careerbuilder, but he felt he'd cobbled together a very complete description. It was three pages long and really captured what he thought was the essence of the job. Going through the job description with George, however, TJ got sort of an uneasy feeling that some of the bullets weren't very well defined. He and

George read them together and there were more occasions than not when TJ sort of shrugged his shoulders not really knowing what the bullet point meant and George moved on.

'Why did this restaurateur make him so nervous?' he wondered.

George finally put the job description down, "but what you're looking for is someone who is really smart."

TJ smiled, but not a smile of happiness, but rather a plaintiff "geez, what the heck" sort of smile.

"Of course I want someone smart, George, that's not a hiring criteria."

"Not 'smart,' TJ," George scolded. "'Really smart'" and he emphasized the words.

George could see the pained look on TJ's face. "Okay," he said, "like Jonathan," and George pointed over to one his busboys. "Jonathan graduated from Drake with a degree in accounting. He was here during his undergraduate work and has stayed on. He'll undoubtedly leave someday to start a bigger career, but he's really smart and I never have to tell him to do anything, he can help with the books, he can help with planning, he can build the order, calculate profits and he's also someone customers can have a conversation with, and some even turn to him for advice."

"He has an undergraduate degree in accounting?" TJ asked. "Did he just graduate or something?"

"Yes, a degree in accounting. Not bad, eh? He graduated about a year-and-a-half ago and is still thinking about going back for his masters. Privately, I'm pushing him to do that," and George smiled broadly.

'He sure smiles a lot,' TJ thought.

"Wow, what do you pay him?" TJ asked.

"That's the second criteria," George said. "Hire really smart people and then pay them really well."

"So, that's it. What about skills?"

"Of course that's not it," George said sort of feigning some frustration.

TJ was relieved because he thought he'd wasted a whole lot of time.

"You need to hire really happy too," George said.

"What?" TJ asked and was almost about to come out of his chair. Behind his "What?" were all the questions he'd be asked at Trill Industries about why he'd decided to spend weeks in a restaurant with George, why he'd listened to the janitor. He saw in the millisecond between his question and George's response his career. He envisioned himself diving head first over a cliff and as he closed his eyes to watch his body splat against the wet rocks below George spoke in sort of a chirpy, sing-songy, rhythmic ditty.

"TJ, you hire really smart, really happy people and pay them really well."

TJ watched as he hit head first and then the rest of his body followed the head into a bloody mass. At the very end of the scenario his Johnston and Murphy, on his right foot, for some reason, spun around on its heel, stood for a moment and then silently skittered down the boulder and into the churning turf.

"No one to blame but myself," TJ muttered.

"What?" George asked.

"I've got no one to blame but myself, George. I'm sorry. Great lunches, but I'm in a world of hurt here and your offering me...me...fairy tales."

George was quiet.

"I'm sorry," TJ repeated. "I don't mean to be mean, but my world is crashing down around me and I don't know what to do."

"You need results," George said. "TJ, I've owned this restaurant for almost 40 years. I get results. You hire really smart, really happy people and you pay them really well. That's part of the magic."

TJ rested his forehead in his palms.

"You know anyone whose really smart and in your industry?" George asked.

"Listen, think about that for a minute. Let me go wait on these customers" and George pointed to a line that had suddenly developed and snaked out the door. "Don't leave I'll be right back."

What George was asking really wasn't that hard for TJ. He pulled out his tablet and started perusing the company's access to monster.com's database. He searched for "sales," for "VP of Sales," and for "Sales manager." In no time he had 14 resumes he thought would fill the bill. To be safe he went to his LinkedIn account and pulled another 6. '20 even. Perfect.'

George was still busy, but the line was dwindling. TJ really didn't know why he stayed. Perhaps it was morbid curiosity. Maybe he realized his career was ending in slow motion right before his eyes and he'd never had the experience. Maybe after his leap off the cliff and onto the rocks, learned helplessness set in and he knew that even if he went another direction he'd be using even more time. So he waited. He looked at the really smart people he'd pulled up. He checked his Facebook account. He looked at his work email, shook his head and closed the email.

"Think of any?" George asked as he pulled back his chair.

TJ handed the tablet to George and then had to show him quickly how to thumb through the resumes.

'This just gets better and better,' he thought and plopped himself back into his chair.

"So, where'd you find all these?" George asked.

TJ explained what he had done, but tried to embellish his search a bit. He was a bit too defeated and exhausted to exert a lot of effort on embellishment, but he gave it some effort.

Unfortunately for TJ, or perhaps fortunately, George wasn't buying any of it.

"No good," George said.

"What?" TJ responded his voice somewhat more irritated than his earlier "What?" "Ok, maybe I didn't spend all day and night on this, but I have other stuff to do. I can't spend weeks and weeks trying to find someone. These were the cream of the crop I could find with the time I had while you were actually running your business."

"Then the crop's no good," George responded and TJ was a little surprised George appeared to have gotten his allusion. "You cannot tell me if any of these people are really smart and if they are not you simply have the cream of a really poor crop."

"How do I know, then, George?"

"You already interviewed a bunch of sales managers in your industry and others you know, right?" George asked, but it was a rhetorical question.

Even so, TJ listed off four or five people.

"Call them back. Tell them you're looking for a super-salesperson, but you want someone who is the smartest person they know. And, just like last time you wait until you start hearing the same names over and over. Then, you call that person and you talk with him and...or her...and you find out from that person, too, who they know who is really smart. And when you find at least five names that three different people give you as being really smart you quit calling and come back to see me. Understand?"

"George, I'm running out of time."

"No," George said, but it wasn't a comment; it was a command. "No, you never run out of time for hiring. Hire right, or don't hire. That's the rule."

TJ left the restaurant, but he wasn't happy. 'This is garbage,' he thought when he got back to his office and checked his emails. Later that afternoon, though, he picked up the phone and called Tony Trill.

He didn't hear back from Dr. Trill until late that evening. TJ was just sitting down to another t.v. dinner when his cell phone rang.

Tony listened to TJ explain what he had been doing even though TJ felt a bit awkward, and he sort of changed some things, because he couldn't imagine what Tony would have said had he known his entire Des Moines operation hinged on some Greek restaurant owner, "you know the friend of the janitor." TJ felt he was lost. Trill, however, didn't skip a beat, but began giving TJ contact information to "five of the smartest people I know."

"And," Dr. Trill added, "you can call Shirley and then call Jack tonight as they're both on the west coast and so it's not too late."

"Thanks, Tony," TJ said as he hung up.

'Well, he probably thinks I've lost my mind, but at least he humored me,' He pushed his t.v. dinner aside. It was hardly worth eating anyway and went to his phone.

The next couple of days TJ spent dialing, talking and tracking down one lead after another.

In his mind with each phone call he kept hearing "Tick-tock," "Tick-tock," Tick-tock" and the sound of the clock was growing louder.

"There's a guy in Georgia you should talk to…"

"Tick-tock."

"Definitely call Matt. He should be at his Aspen home this time of year. His number is..."

"Tick-tock."

"Don't know that you could get him, but Paul with Ashworth Airlines would be worth a conversation. His background is all software, management and sales."

"Tick-tock."

"You want Kelly. She'll blow you away with all that she brings to the table."

His list grew from Dr. Trill's original to about 16 before he got his second hit. The third hit on the same name followed two calls later. And then another name came up a second time a call after that.

On Friday he walked back into George's carrying four resumes and two alternates.

"Perfect," George replied. "You have really smart people, right?"

TJ nodded.

"How do you know?"

TJ immediately laid out the process he'd been through to acquire his list.

"Perfect. Now, you need to call each one and that's even if you've already talked with them."

"Okay," TJ said. "I'll do a phone interview and then bring in the top two for a panel."

"Not yet," George responded. "Call them. Remember, you want to hire really happy as well. That's all you're calling for. You want to find out if they're really happy."

TJ sat in front of George. He thought maybe George was possibly intoxicated.

"So I want really smart," TJ began, "and I want really happy."

George grinned and nodded his head. "Yes, yes. Exactly. Really smart and really happy people are the best."

"Okay, George, I'll bite, how will I know in a phone call if someone is really happy?" TJ asked.

"You know who is happy and works for me, right?"

"Yes, George, but I'm in here almost everyday and I get to see them working and interacting with your customers."

"Yep. The other problem is I only hire really happy, so they're all really happy. Much harder over the phone, but you'll know the moment they pick up the phone just like you knew about my staff the first day you walked in here. If they sound bored, if you get the sense their handshake would be a dead fish, if there's no excitement in their voice, if they sound exhausted, if they sound brusque or mean, if they have layers of people in front of them just to get to them. You'll know. You'll know"

TJ felt as though the advice was razor-thin in terms of his ability to discern over the phone whether someone was "happy," but he couldn't deny the fact that George seemed to have this process down pretty good and he was a bit nervous and a bit anxious to see how this all would work out. He wished he'd checked for "happy" in the preceding phone call with the couple he'd talked with making his rounds to find "really smart," but he'd check again.

When he got back to his office he closed his door and began making phone calls.

"Good afternoon, Liken Brothers, this is Art Messer," the voice on the other end of the line said.

"Art, TJ, with Trill Industries and I'm calling to talk with Robert Madison please."

"Please hold."

"Good afternoon, this is Emily Preston, Mr. Madison's personal assistant, "Can I help you?"

"Yes, this is Thomas Johnson, TJ, with Trill Industries and I'm calling to speak with Mr. Madison please."

"May I ask the nature of your call."

"Well, it's a bit personal, but I was really wanting to talk with Mr. Madison about Trill Industries and the direction we're heading to see if he might have some insights into..."

To get to Robert took TJ about 8 or 9 minutes and then Robert answered the phone with "This is Mr. Madison," a voice that sounded a little exhausted said, "how may I help you?" Robert Madison was at once extremely formal, very professional and a bit off-putting. 'He doesn't sound that happy' TJ thought, had a brief conversation with Robert and hung up.

The next call TJ made went to South America, Venezuela. Marcus Sparkman was an interesting and very upbeat person, but he didn't express much of an interest in talking about TJ's opportunity, although he thanked TJ profusely for calling, was excited to be considered and "was most excited to have my name in this elite circle" TJ had put together.

"Hello, this is Mumps" a peppy voice on the other end of the line answered.

"Yes, this is Thomas Johnson, TJ, with Trill Industries and I'd like to speak to Charlene Trisco please."

"This is she Thomas Johnson, TJ, but it's always Cheryl" the voice on the phone responded and he could since the playfulness even without her play on his introduction. "Or, preferably, Mumps."

"And it's always TJ," TJ responded.

"Mumps" was a nickname Charlene had picked up in grade school when she had mumps and the symptoms of a swollen face lingered on for over a year. The doctors were initially concerned and she was out of school for weeks on end, but eventually even the doctors quit worrying about her "condition." By the time the swelling went down she was "Mumps." She owned the nickname and it became her. She liked it a lot better than Charlene, Cheryl, or Char anyway.

He hung up 35 minutes later, realizing he felt as though they had spoken for only a few minutes.

His only worry was her compensation was already pretty far out there and that was before TJ worked his formula on an incentive. Other than that he was ready to make an offer. He thought about it, but decided he'd better talk it over with George.

'Maybe you should include Javier too,' the little sarcastic voice said in the back of his head as he walked down the steps to George's restaurant. TJ had decided George and Javier were the horses he was going to ride to the end of this race, whatever that "end" looked like, so he'd muffled his frustration and dampened his attitude and brightened his mood. Plus he was way pumped about Mumps.

"Hey, George," he hollered at George's wave.

"TJ, what can I do for you today?"

"Would you mind if I just grabbed a coffee and waited for you."

"Could be a while," George said.

"Okay," TJ responded and got his coffee and made his way to a table. He worked through some of his emails, but mostly watched George and his restaurant staff. He never saw anyone with a cross word. There were lots of things like "Yes sir, I'll get that for you" and "Right away, mam that's right over here." Everyone was moving to satisfy George's customers. Eventually, George made his way to TJ's table.

"Big smile, from Mr. TJ. You got something good for me?"

TJ acknowledged the ribbing, but he did have something good for George.

They talked about Mumps for a few minutes. TJ felt she was just what he needed.

"So, what's the problem?" George asked.

"With incentives she's probably 100K above where I want to pay," TJ confided in his...friend.

He was surprised when he thought about Javier, or when he thought about George. He could remember having help that was first generation Italian, or what he thought was Italian, or he had a guy he knew once that was first generation German, but he had never thought of anyone of color, or anyone who was a 'foreigner' as a friend. Javier and George he thought of as friends.

"No. Not a problem," George said. "Remember, the final part of the equation 'and pay them really well?'"

"Hire really smart, really happy people and pay them really well," George said, but TJ, with George's accent, again felt George sort of sang it rather than said it.

"Hire really smart, really happy people and pay them really well," TJ repeated.

"You're almost there, TJ," George said, "but you have to do one final thing before you consider the offer."

"What's that, George?"

"You're hiring by what your job description says you need, right?"

TJ nodded.

"Ok, but that's only a list of tasks and as we went through it, it's probably not a great list of tasks."

TJ sort of fumbled with his plagiarized job description.

"Look, TJ, you kind of have a decent enough job description," George said, "but I don't get the sense your description is what you need." George went on to explain in greater detail what his most recent riddle meant. TJ listened intently but also became aware that he was beginning to get comfortable talking with George and understanding the deeper meaning behind the riddles. He also remembered a conversation he had had with George a while back about exactly what George was talking about.

"What you are looking for in this whole thing is something another customer in a similar predicament of mine calls a model."

"A model," TJ repeated as more of a question than an affirmation. "I remember us talking about that briefly weeks ago."

"Yes," George said. "To build a model you do what you've already done and find two or three people who are currently performing the function and performing it at such a high level that they are really superstars. Is this sounding familiar, TJ? Remember when I told you to call your sales superstars?"

TJ of course immediately remembered all the early phone calls he'd made and the attributes he'd listed.

"Remember, they're the folks a manager turns to and says I cannot live without this person."

TJ nodded his head. "I remember, George."

He remembered well the superstars, the people who, when their names were mentioned at an event, one would have thought an orchestra would play in the background.

TJ knew the exact superstars George was talking about.

"You called them and talked with them, TJ. You asked them how they go about doing their jobs. Asked them for the top four or five things they think they do maybe differently or better than anyone else. And then I know you were amazed because the top four or five things they do differently or better than everyone else were all essentially the same. Those are the attributes you found in Mumps."

"Of course," TJ said. "That's the missing piece. That's the rest of this magic."

"You know, George, I feel a bit like the Karate Kid," TJ confided.

"How so?" George smiled.

"I painted the fence, or wax on wax off, or whatever, but you're Mr. Miyagi."

George laughed at that one. "Whatever you think, TJ."

"I think you have most the magic," George said. "You've essentially done the work already. Mumps sounds like a real strong possibility." And TJ quickly pieced together his model in his mind and felt Mumps hit all the criteria he had found weeks before in his conversations. She was really smart and she was really happy. He was only missing one component and then he was done.

He needed to talk to Trill. He knew Mumps could set his world on fire. He had to get Trill's approval on the salary. He left George's restaurant and walked back to his office.

He dialed Trill's office and no sooner did Candace answer then he remembered Trill would be out of the office on vacation, a "photo" safari of all things, for the next few weeks. There were limited ways to get in touch with him.

He felt himself running in slow motion again after a ship leaving a dock. 'No-o-o-o-o...' he saw his character saying. 'What now?' he thought.

"Darn it," he said as he hung up the phone.

"What, TJ?" Javier asked.

"Oh, sorry, Javier," TJ said. "I didn't realize I said that out loud."

"Not to worry, TJ. Anything I can help with?"

"I don't think so, Javier. I just needed to get approval for a salary from Dr. Trill and now he's out for a few weeks and this isn't an emergency and so it'll just have to wait."

"Whew-boy, do you have weeks to wait?" Javier said without really meaning it to sound probably as threatening or as accusatory as it did.

TJ looked up a Javier.

"Sorry, TJ, but I love numbers and the numbers on our ship don't seem to say to me 'wait weeks.' And plus, Tony, gave you the helm and said 'steer,' so I think you should steer."

Javier was real good at making a suggestion, providing input and then disappearing. He did that here much to TJ's chagrin. TJ had two thoughts: 'he's right' and 'why does Javier think he can call Dr.Trill Tony?'

The following day at lunch TJ explained to George his dilemma and added in Javier's comment.

"Well, you do what you want, but you're a month to 6 weeks away from, what's her name again..."

"Mumps."

"Yeah, Mumps, from being here. You add another couple months to get up to some semblance of speed and pretty soon you're out of time. Time is rarely our friend, TJ," George added.

'Wow, isn't that the truth,' he thought. Time wasn't slipping away from him; it was screaming away. The days had turned to weeks and months and all of a sudden TJ felt his big clock chasing him and ticking, incessantly ticking. He felt like he had a sense of urgency before, but was quickly realizing he felt hyper-urgency was the order of the day.
He called Mumps from his cell phone, extended the offer over the phone, told her "unfortunately he needed her here sooner, rather than later" and so could only give her 48 hours to make a decision and then he'd also need her in

two weeks, even though she could obviously consult with her former employer should she accept his offer. He added lots of preceded by or followed by "I'm sorry," but then simply reemphasized he needed her. The compensation, too, had a substantial at risk component to it, but making goals would be exceptionally rewarding.

"Okay," Mumps responded at the end of his three minute "hurry, up" conversation.

"So, okay, you can get back to me in 48 hours?" TJ asked.

There was a moment's silence. "I can if you want, TJ," Mumps said, "but I said 'okay.'"

"Oh, were you saying okay to the deal?" TJ responded.

She giggled in delight. "TJ, you're hiring me sight unseen, to a deal paying me more than I've ever made, into a company that is simply blowing the doors off in their industry and I'm going to be leading a national sales force and you think there'd be hesitation because I'm what, married to my current boss? And don't take that the wrong way as I love what I'm doing and love this company, but I'm thinking I have to take this opportunity and take it right now from what you've told me."

"With the incentive structure," TJ said.

"What?"

"You mean you'll make more than you've ever made if you reach the goals, right?" TJ hesitantly asked.

"TJ, we're going to make the goals. Send me the offer letter and I'll turn in my notice and see you in two weeks. I won't leave these guys high and dry so you may have to share a little of my time for a little bit, but let's get this done."

'Wow!' TJ thought. 'Wow!' he repeated to himself. She'll be here before Dr. Trill gets back.

'Oh my god,' he thought as the offer he'd extended to Mumps was bigger, richer and different than anything Trill Industries had ever tried and Dr. Trill had to approve it and he wouldn't even be in the office before she started. 'What were you thinking?' he screamed at himself.

She sure made decisions quickly was TJ's other thought. That's good. This is good. It will work out.

Two weeks passed in a moment. Mumps and he spoke on the phone at least once daily and emails and IMs flew back-and-forth continuously. He never once reached out to Mumps where he wasn't impressed by her demeanor and he never once reached out where she didn't come back with ideas and criticisms and, what? What would he call it? 'Delight.'

She flew into Des Moines on the weekend before she was to start. It worked out her first day was to be Tuesday, but she arrived in the office Monday and hit the ground as though she'd been there for months. TJ almost immediately ceded the sales team to her and moved on to work on the "leadership stuff" George had told him he needed to be focused on.

Chapter 8
The Good Fight

TJ's life took a dramatic turn with the hiring of Mumps. Eventually he got around to getting her salary approved, but it was an "after-the-fact" affair and he never talked directly with Dr. Trill. Trill didn't question him about the decision, which surprised him a bit, and then made him a tad nervous as Dr. Trill was putting the trust and the responsibility in him. But, as the days turned to weeks TJ began to wonder exactly how he had done everything without Mumps.

Several of his sales force left, but TJ never really was that involved in their leaving. Mumps handled it. All of a sudden, like magic, too, the sales meetings were less about projections and plans and more about results. And the results were inspiring. He had only a few months left before Dr. Trill had previously told him a decision would be made regarding Des Moines, but with the type of progress they were making he felt confident that if a decision were to be made to close an office it wouldn't be Des Moines.

And with Sales "handled," he turned his attention to other neglected parts of the organization, hiring here, coaching there and, yes, and unfortunately, terminating occasionally. Getting the right people on the boat in the right seats with their paddles in the water, rowing in the right direction was all that TJ was about now. George had converted him and he was now an evangelical on the subject. He was also an evangelical on hiring really happy, really smart people and paying them really well.

Too, he was getting out of the office at a reasonable hour as well, which was nice, although Des Moines was still a lonely place. He'd kept the apartment as Trill Industries kept picking up the tab. He talked with Joyce and the kids almost every night and was home most weekends and many times flew out on Wednesday or Thursday and back the following Monday or Tuesday. Sometime in all this back-and-forth traveling between he and Joyce TJ realized he thought of Chicago as "home" and in a year of eventful decisions he knew he was approaching a big one.

The following day end-of-quarter financials landed on his desk. "Christy," he called to his relatively new executive administrative assistant. "Would you double check these numbers?"

"Is there something wrong, TJ?" Christy, who wasn't used to being questioned asked.

"They can't be right," TJ said. "If they are Des Moines is easily the most profitable of all the divisions. We couldn't have gotten here that fast."

"Well, this is the first time I've been asked to check numbers that were too good," she said.

But she knew. She had also questioned the numbers. When she first compiled the numbers from Trill's custom software, grabbed some additional information from Salesforce, and put them in her side-by-side spreadsheet comparing budget to plan to results, she'd double-checked and then double-checked her double-check of her work. She went back and checked the numbers for TJ, but they didn't change.

"They're right, TJ."

"That was really quick."

"I've been through them a half dozen times because I don't believe them either, but they are what they are."

"What they are is phenomenal," TJ responded, but his was something of a rhetorical response.

Trill called later that morning.

"Congrats, TJ. Incredible numbers," Dr. Trill said. "I guess you sort of made a good hiring decision, eh?"

"Well, I guess we did," TJ responded.

"Oh?" Dr. Trill asked the question, TJ wished he hadn't brought up, the question behind his "we" and Dr. Trill's "Oh?" and that was "Who was involved in this process?" But TJ had changed here too and he was no longer an "I," but a "we." He shared the credit and he knew the names of people he was sharing the credit with. And not only their names, but their kids names and activities. He thought about that for the briefest of moments and smiled a satisfied smile.

"I don't know, Tony. This Des Moines thing has been a weird, but enjoyable adventure. I've changed and our numbers are great, but it's so many things."

"Well, I have a few minutes and now I'm doubly curious."

"Ok. I'd start with Javier."

"The 'janitor?'" Trill said matter-of-factly.

Before he could catch himself, TJ said, more emphatically than he would have preferred, "He's not a janitor."

There was an awkward silence for just a minute and then TJ added "sorry, he's the building maintenance person, but whatever we want to title him yes, Javier."

"And if you love the janitor part, you're going to absolutely die over the next person involved. George Hatzigiannakis," and TJ said the last name hats-a-gee-a-nak-us as though he'd spoken it his entire life. "He's a first generation Greek restaurateur who is simply brilliant. Javier introduced us."

"Amazing,. Really?" Dr. Trill said. "So, what did George Hatzigiannakis," and TJ was momentarily a bit stunned at how easily Dr. Trill pronounced the name, "share with you?"

"Hire really happy, really smart people and pay them really well," TJ laughed at how easily he'd picked up George's cadence and rhythm. "He shared with me building a model, a composite sketch of not top performers, but performance superstars. When I asked my questions I was comparing Mumps against the composite sketch of Superman, or woman, salespeople. She aligned perfectly in almost every category. Most importantly, when I spoke with her it was like talking to...I don't know how to describe it..."

"Happy," Dr. Trill added.

"Happy," TJ repeated, "upbeat, can do, get out of my way, look out. Just absolutely phenomenal."

"The magic's in the model, Tony," TJ added.

"Model," Dr. Trill said and there was this moment of silence as both mulled the word. "That's a very interesting concept, TJ."

"What makes it interesting is how well it works. I've hired three more leaders and all of them came in here and are just flat out turning this deal around."

"Turned," Dr. Trill said.

"What?" TJ said.

"That's why I called, TJ," Dr. Trill said. "Congratulations. Des Moines is staying in the fold."

TJ sighed a deep sigh.

"Not exactly the response I had expected," Dr. Trill said. "Maybe if I talk with you about the compensation increase and title change I have in mind, you'll get a bit more excited."

"Dr. Trill," TJ started, "I cannot begin to express my gratitude for all the opportunity, especially after I failed so miserably in Chicago,"

"We TJ," Tony interrupted. "We failed in Chicago."

"Granted," TJ said, "but…"

"There's always a but, isn't there TJ?" Dr. Trill said and sort of chuckled.

"Yes, sir, there often is. But Chicago is home and Joyce is there and my kids are there."

"And you should be there," like a married couple, Dr. Trill was finishing TJ's sentences.

"Yes sir, I should be there. So I guess that to say I've had a fabulous run with your company."

"Our company TJ," Dr. Trill interrupted again.

"Yes, sir, of course, but I need to go home and work on some other stuff for a bit."

"President and CEO." Dr. Trill said.

"What?"

"That's the job title," Dr. Trill said. "My position. I'm retiring. The board wants a visionary. I'll be acting as Chair Emeritus, whatever the heck that means. About double your salary with additional stock and additional options. It's yours to run, TJ."

TJ usually had a fairly firm grasp of his surroundings. He always had made it a point to have a plan and work the plan. He could remember the very few times he'd been thrown off stride. Trill's offer knocked him down.

"Think about it, TJ," Dr. Trill said. "We need you, your ideas, but mostly your ability to change and to change the organization. Take us to the next level."

TJ thought for a moment and was preparing to say "I'll think about it. Thank you," But what came out was "No."

Now it was Dr. Trill's turn to say "what?"

"Tony, I'm sorry. My experience in Des Moines has been stunning. But I have a family and the offer your making is telling me that I'd need to go back to working like I worked before and I'm sorry but that simply isn't going to happen again. So, with respect, no."

"No, TJ, the point is I don't want you to work like you did before; I want you to work like you do now. I want you hiring really smart, really happy people and if you have to pay them really well, let the results speak for themselves.

That's what I want. That's what we want. And we want models. And we want your ideas. That's the leadership we need."

There was another moment of silence before Dr. Trill spoke again, "Okay, TJ, here's what I want you to do. Go to Chicago. Take whatever time you need. Talk with Joyce. Talk with the kids. Make a decision as a family. That's the way you should be making these decisions anyway. You know that now. Get back with me in a month and then if you say no, I'll walk away. But understand Des Moines wasn't a test for you; it was the final experience. Javier and George and I have been training our managers and leaders for years."

"You have?"

"Yep. Did you ever ask Javier what he was doing before being our janitor?"Dr. Trill said.

"No."

"Ever look in his personnel file?"

"Uh, no."

"Of course not. He's a really smart janitor who I hired out of the Sloan Business School when he was teaching futurism type junk. He brought all that to Des Moines. George was serendipitous. Javier stumbled across him. But when we found George the whole shooting match came together and we decided to create the Trill Industries Academy."

"I thought that was an urban legend."

"It is. You just lived through it. You just embraced it. You just took it to a whole different level. TJ, I'm so right about you taking this job I can't even begin to imagine a scenario where I'm going to allow you to turn it down, so if you come back to me in a month or two and you say 'okay, Trill, but I'm working from my house in my pajamas and video conferencing everywhere,' I'm probably going to say 'sounds terrific.' You're the right guy in the right place and at the right time. Besides you're really happy and really smart and I'm going to pay you really well."

TJ laughed. "Okay, I'll think about it."

"Good, talk with you in a month."

"I can have a decision for you after the weekend."

"A month, TJ. Take your time. I'm going no where."

"Okay, I'll think about it and get back to you in a month."

The two men hung up. TJ sat for a moment in his office. Javier, as if on cue, appeared at the door.

"You alright, TJ?" he asked.

"You know I am, Javier."

"Congratulations, sir."

"I haven't accepted."

"I hope you do. We'll make a great team."

"You going to stay then?" TJ asked.

"You don't know everything yet," Javier responded emptying the trash and wheeling his cart out of the office.

"That's why you call him Tony, isn't it Javier?" TJ asked.

"He's been to the house," Javier responded.

"Of course he has," TJ said and clicked his mouse, opened Outlook Calendar and calendared a month from this incredible day. He sat momentarily looking at the newly saved appointment and then closed the cover on his tablet putting it to sleep. He grabbed a couple of stacks from his desk, tossed them into his satchel and headed for the airport.

"Talk with you in a month," Javier called to him as he exited the building.

TJ turned around to see his friend smiling, always smiling.

"A month," he shouted back, waved, and turned toward the parking garage.

Epilogue

If you're ever in downtown Des Moines, under the parking garage on 7th Street sits a little restaurant, Mr. Filet Steakhouse. At the head of the speed line is George Hatzigiannakis. Serving baked potatoes or French fries is the younger George. At the register many times is George's wife, Mary. Simeon Mantzavinos, who used to greet many of the women coming into the restaurant as "Bridget Bardot," passed away many years ago at the age of 44, taken from us by lung cancer.

Other parts of the preceding story are composite sketches of various people I've met and worked with in my more than two decades of doing this human resources thing. I generally chose names from people I liked a bunch and used them in this piece because they were easy to remember, but they were also very happy and very smart.

What I've found are the tools I discuss in the preceding pages work and work at an unparalleled level. I've also found hiring really happy, really smart people and paying them really well is THE absolute magic.

According to Bill Taylor (at http://blogs.hbr.org/taylor/2011/02/hire_for_attitude_train_for_sk.html) and many others (like, as I remember, Jody Hoffer Gittell in the excellent book *The Southwest Airlines Way*) I've read Southwest Airlines' hiring mantra is "hire for attitude and train for skill." They don't advocate hiring incompetent clowns as pilots simply because they're happy. They wouldn't have much of a business if they did. None of us would. But happiness isn't usually (999 out of a 1,000 times) something we can train, or coach or counsel. Happiness is an innate desire to make lemonade out lemons, to see rainbows and ponies, to wake up thankful to have another opportunity to make a difference in someone's life. Hiring happy is the magic bullet to making a company phenomenal.

Competence and intelligence are also critical. I never really liked job descriptions. They always made me feel like a basketball playing chicken. When I was a kid, many moons ago, I went to the county fair one year and there was a chicken in a cage with a basketball hoop at one end of the cage. You slipped a coin into a slot and a bell rang and a little orange "basketball" came out of a chute and that chicken started pecking at that ball until the ball went through the basket, another bell rang and some bird seed came out another chute. That basketball playing chicken would have kept pecking at that ball until she died of exhaustion. Her sole goal was to get to the bird seed.

I look at job descriptions and most incentive plans and I see the basketball playing chicken. All this HR stuff is sort of disrespectful in this way. That's where my model, and it's probably not a unique concept I invented, comes from. In fact in Eric Herrenkohl's excellent work, *How to Hire A-Players*, he has essentially the same concept, "A-Player profiles" (but with more pages).

Take not "the very best," but the really powerful, over-the-top performers you have in an area and you interview them and you listen very closely for the things they do differently, or monumentally better, than the next level of performer. And then you develop a composite sketch of that ideal.

And, I apologize as my intent wasn't to write this book when I started my research a couple of decades ago, so I didn't keep copious notes about sources, but I remember reading where one of these top performing superstars can out work "average" by seven times. More importantly I've seen where they do. At State National Bank one of our superstar tellers averaged seven times as many transactions as the next highest "average" performer. Think about that for a moment—a company full of people producing seven times the average for an industry.

Then you develop behavior-based questions focused solely on testing how closely the person across the table fits your model. When you hand a candidate a job description, he or she is answering questions, painting a picture of what you want to see, what they think meets the attributes you're looking for, which not surprisingly, 99 out of 100 times, is your job description.

When you ask questions of a candidate and you are comparing their answers to your model, they're still painting a picture, but rather than painting you the picture they think you want to see, they're painting you a picture of their reality and you're comparing it against what you need. The only caveat to this process I've found is that a little difference makes a lot of difference. What I mean by that is if you have a candidate who is "pretty" close to your model, but just not quite there, then you should move on. You want someone who aligns darn close. What's the difference between "pretty" and "darn?" That's probably something, with apologies, you'll have to experience.

One thing too, alluded to in TJ's adventures is the ability to hire patiently and fire quickly. If someone doesn't fit, folks, someone doesn't fit. We have to get them off the boat, out or our bus, or whatever analogy you prefer, very quickly. Unfortunately. We've made a mistake. There's nothing easy about admitting to that mistake, but there's not a way we're going to right that wrong either.

So, packed in this story of TJ, Javier, Dr. Trill, Mumps, Joyce, George, et al. is the hiring magic I've found in my life's experience in HR. The sing-songy ditty that George tells TJ, "hire really happy, really smart people and pay them really well," is probably the most powerful hiring criteria I can share with anyone who will listen. Most don't listen as they think the same as was TJ's initial reaction "it's sing-songy" and silly. If someone will feel better with its addition, he or she could add "really hardworking" to the preceding three. But I really don't worry so much about that one.

And, if you go to Mr. Filet, and George hasn't retired, you'll get the greatest steak in the Midwest for a really good price. But, George, like with all my characters, is a composite sketch of a number of different people that have touched and influenced me throughout my life. He probably won't share any hiring philosophies with you, but he will share delicious food, great atmosphere and better than fair price. And say "hi" to my friend for me because he is definitely a part of my story, beyond the hiring science, that is absolutely real. In fact I've always thought of George as less a friend and more my brother. A lot, too, the way I felt about Simeon.

Thank you for reading. If you have comments, questions, concerns, corrections, errata, need me to come speak about my work, please direct those queries, concerns, corrections, errata, needs to my personal blog, http://hrhiring.wordpress.com/, where you can also find the full manuscript (not this fable) of my work before I made it readable (although it is free at this website). Too, you're welcome to email me at rcastle263@gmail.com.

Within this manuscript at my blog is an example model. At my blog, too, is another example model. We cannot find something when we don't know what we're searching for; models refine and direct our search. Good searching and good luck.

Thank you for reading.

Visit me sometime at http://hrhiring.wordpress.com. I'm not a very active blogger at the moment, but I post cool things when I create them or run across them.

Have questions? Or, if I can help, or to report errata, please contact me at

rcastle263@gmail.com.,

@RexCastle on twitter, or

join me on Facebook, LinkedIn or google+, or whatever the next "thing" is (please let me know you received this invite through my book).

www.ingramcontent.com/pod-product-compliance
Lightning Source LLC
Chambersburg PA
CBHW071229170526
45165CB00003B/1046